EVERYTHING

IS

BURNING

Also by Gerald Stern

EVERYTHING

IS

BURNING

poems

Gerald Stern

W. W. Norton & Company
New York London

For information about permission to reproduce selections from
this book, write to Permissions, W. W. Norton & Company, Inc.
500 Fifth Avenue, New York, NY 10110

Manufacturing by The Courier Companies, Inc.
Book design by Anna Oler
Production Manager: Amanda Morrison

Library of Congress Cataloging-in-Publication Data

Stern, Gerald, date.
  Everything is burning : poems / Gerald Stern.—1st ed.
      p. cm.
  ISBN 0-393-06055-1
  I. Title.
  PS3569.T3888E95 2005
  811'.54—dc22

                                        2005004430

W. W. Norton & Company, Inc.
500 Fifth Avenue, New York, N.Y. 10110
www.wwnorton.com

W. W. Norton & Company Ltd.
Castle House, 75/76 Wells Street, London W1T 3QT

1 2 3 4 5 6 7 8 9 0

For my grandchildren
Rebecca, Julia, Dylan

Contents

1

III

EVERYTHING

IS

BURNING

1

A Google of Geese

A google of geese running after the chunks of bread,
pigeons around them, in and out like sparrows,
ducks moving in, the chiefest Magnificat, God
sort of, in a light blue T-shirt and blue pants
scattering seven-grain from the inside of a warehouse
for the geese to eat as once the Jews in Exodus
that sweet tasting bread, be it thistle, be it the wind
that blew the fruit, the finches and loaves of the sky,
ducks and pigeons too, those were the sausage-eaters,
those were the drinkers of blood, the hand was kind.

La Pergola

Finally daisies and tomatoes, I have settled for
that and bushes more important than fruit and
flowers and one gray squirrel running back and forth on
the fence and leaping onto the humbled sunflower,
how deep it bows, the tomatoes are only green
and as we speak I am out there bending over,
making a bouquet of daisies, you can
count them, I have five fedoras, there in
the back room of La Pergola I take a
break from eating kasha and varnishkas
to primp and glow, damn the bushes, damn
the bald daisies, stinking blue vase, stinking dixie cup.

The Cup

Leaves on the frozen floor and Aristotle
lying face down on top of the patchwork pillows
and one glass vase with the water gone and the pebbles
rattling and that narcissus on a chair
forced into life and then forced out, the cup
yellow, edged with red, the name *poeticus*.

E.P. 1

Nothing matters but the quality of the affection,
neither the bicyclist riding by in her black baseball cap
nor the three trees I planted in my backyard,
I should say four counting the small apple
nailed to my neighbor's fence, nor can I
discount the memory he had of Ferdie and Fordie,
prick and snob though he was. But I never trusted his
paradise, it was too literary, nor his
final confession, nor what he said to Ginsberg—
imagine, imagine—nor, ah, the endless self-pity
taking the place of character, so un-Kung
after all, although there were two paradises,
weren't there, lying master that he was, and
one was a shut garden of pear trees, dancing Nancy.

E.P. 11

He died I was in Somerville, New Jersey or
nearabouts. I practically ran a community
college and called a kind of memorial, the nursing
students alone took notes, they would take notes
while Jesus was drowning, wouldn't they? I read the Pity
and Valasek read the Usury, we were still taken
by the hoarfrost and the staggering ants;
and it was a large room but it was shameful
there were no flowers, neither lynx nor Bassarids
to accompany him into his hypostasis.

E.P. III

I meant the personal and the social,
or call it the historical if you like,
I mean I meant there was a personal paradise
and there was a larger one, be it aesthetic,
be it political, theological, beauty was
not only difficult, it was impossible, meester
Pound, for Europe was poisoned. How you like Europe
now? How you like Dubya? Wyoming hath need of thee.

The 18th Book Fair

An embarassment of poverty, we waded into
thousands of new volumes, the great-grandchildren
praising the great-greats and I was sitting
facing Hayden Carruth passing a Picayune
back and forth comparing the taste to something
between a Lucky Strike and a Gauloise
though we were both gasping for breath and he
could hardly write, his hand was shaking so much,
but to our credit we were peeking and I said
"Listen to this line," and he, "This is the
best death of Hector I ever read,"
in *plein air* in downtown Miami Mitch
Kaplan put together for the 18th Book Fair.

Berries of Death

Berries of death, they hang from shabby branches
and have the lustre of tomatoes but not
rotten tomatoes, sitting on the cold ground
still brilliant, full of death; oh ugly Portuguese
that ate them on the way to the Azores, cramping
and yelling, crows that drop down to eat the berries
shitting in the sky, stupefied crows.

Albatross 1

Please listen, there's a thing back there I killed
that's spiritual and has two wings like anything
we love forever—take the pigeon, take the
bluebird—I would rather walk with a cane
than hurt a bluebird; I would kill anyone who stuffed
a full-grown frog into a mason jar
and threw him from a third floor window, the glass
cutting his body, penetrating his mouth
and eyes. You have to get down there and kill
the frog yourself before you run upstairs
and beat him, holding him half out the window, let his
name be erased for the thing back there.

Those Are Saucers
That Were His Eyes

Me and my critic, me and my wife, a dog that
doesn't love me, he and his bloodshot eyes, his
curling lip, the flaps above the teeth that
he pulls back, the belly he crawls on, the stink
of his mouth, is his name Sandy? Does he
say "arf?" Does that mean I am a dog? Does that
mean *Je suis un autre?* Does that mean "now that you have
new lenses you can see my saucers perfectly?" Oh
Annie my love, my teeth have a life of their own.
Help me out of this. During the Cuban War
they let us kill the poets. We had thumbs then,
up, down, man's best friend must either
growl or kill. We have our own president,
not enough birds! Too much obfuscation!
Who cares about your life, bastard hero?

Dead Bat

for Christy Baldyga

Dead bat, I slipped a cardboard underneath him
and held it at arm's length, although his own arm
begged, sort of reached out like Demosthenes,
arguing for his life, whatever broom had
brought him down and that way he ended his pleading.

Never Went to Birdland

Never went to Birdland, so what, went to the Y,
danced all night for a quarter, girls sat down
on bridge chairs, can't remember if they were smoking,
men wore jackets and ties, I know the name of
one, I'll call her Doris—that was her name—
her grandfather was a rabbi from Bialystock
and over ninety—she was twenty, I was
twenty-one, I guess, he had to be born
before the Crimean War; and who were the gangs
that built the wide-gauge railroad tracks that reached
the Urals in 1860? He was only
five feet tall, his hands you can't imagine
nor what the sofa was like and what our struggle was.

Dr. Dunn

The small white coffin I tried talking about over and over

The roomful of cousins staring at me my large green eyes

Dr. Dunn coming by day after day to help my sick mother

No one could survive the Depression without a small
tragedy of her own

The word "cut" as in "I got cut yesterday" followed by
sadness

The only car on the street my father's 1933 wire-spoked
Chevrolet

No pills in the house I went back to it forty years later

Thought was his provenance, love his regimen.

Suzanne

This much I know, I walked through the scraggly wood
behind the Italian restaurant on the highway
south of Camden, my former girlfriend Joanne,
her sister, her white-haired mother, her niece Suzanne,
and we were waiting for dinner; Suzanne and I
walked over the glass and the burning rubbish
downhill from the restaurant and when we came back
her mother was furious for it was dark and
disgusting out there and she was holding a lilac
she picked up from the fire and I was crestfallen,
the way I get, my neck was crimson, Suzanne
was smelling the burned lilac, she was seven.

Tenderness

for Linda Gregg

The whole idea of tenderness, she says,
should be tried out on the redbud first, she says,
and all the bees who eat there in the sunlight
should be my object first though she came earlier,
she of whom I speak, where no one saw her
and stripped a twig as though it were a honey locust
and stared at the bees the way as in the hospital
she stared, she said, at a middle-Easterner
though maybe she said *near*-Easterner and there was
only softness and delicacy in his eyes
and there was nothing of harm done to the tree
though when *I* looked at the bees they were disturbed
and I just walked away from their curling bodies
and sat on the brick walk so I could hear
the Chinese cancer patient waiting to be burned,
eighty or ninety years old, singing to his wife
sotto voce yet the whole room heard it,
they were so close together on First Avenue,
Linda getting ready for her fourth burning,
the bees insatiable, the redbud groaning.

The Snow on the River

Snow on the river is my guess though any
change in temperature would do and sometimes
filth alone and as for the cracking, that comes
now in March and sometimes even earlier,
one cloud bumping into another as
we used to say, two sticks curling, then exploding,
some seamy actor from the '50s mixing
one smoke with another, his gum popping.

The Gulls

The other side of the reservoir uphill
from the tennis court he had to take two streetcars
to get there he was running again and they were
screaming only because there was no food though
you'd think they'd go to the river Allegheny,
leftover rotten fish and floating pork—
look, a gull, look, look, a man running
uphill, downhill, he catches his breath that way
he is a fool, he imitates the gulls by
lifting his arms and floating, the other place
he runs is on an abandoned race track called
the Oval, no gulls there, a pack of dogs
getting closer, the moon as he recalls
in one end of the Oval, the sun in the other,
since that is the way they shared the sky, dogs
were distant and vicious then, everything was hungry.

Dog That I Am

I sing for the similarity and I moan for
the face, dog that I am, whippet that I was,
her face of exhaustion, lines in her forehead, her hair
uncombed and unbrushed, the wind in her eyes, she
    could be
from Thrace, from Denmark, I could be from Rome
waiting for her command, I could be from
Egypt and dogging her and I could be from
Spain, a silky wearing a sweater and she with
a scarf at her throat and another one over her mouth
bending to hold my face up, wearing a herringbone
overcoat with deep pockets and buttons
circa 1940, 1950 with
black Westies on her feet and neat little
lapets at the top, the neighborhood of Skinker
near a birch tree, only an accident,
just a mistake—I scream outright at the likeness.

Sylvia

Across a space peopled with stars I am
laughing while my sides ache for existence
it turns out is profound though the profound
because of time it turns out is an illusion
and all of this is infinitely improbable
given the space, for which I gratefully lie
in three feet of snow making a shallow grave
I would have called an angel otherwise and
think of my own rapturous escape from
living only as dust and dirt, little sister.

11

Hemingway's House

I don't want to go to Hemingway's house,
let him come to mine, walk in and we'll do
The Killers at my kitchen table, he with his
back to the Japanese maple, me with my back
to the Maytag, ginger ale for one, white rum
the other; the dragon and the mayfly, death and the
    knowledge of death,
Monk and Bartók all the same to me.

Just Say Goodbye to Mother

What about Damon Runyon, his cloth booties,
the pineapple upside-down cake his mother
burned while caramelizing, the shower in the basement
that after all the wrenches and wrenching was only
a trickle, and after 1898 he
had to live without his mother—oh
the white boys in the Philippines—and carry
his gear on his back and you may not believe it
the sweet and milky songs they sang and what
Samuel Clemens said about *that* war
or how I banged on the door at the post office
and someone met me with his finger wagging
again and again from 1941 to
1945, my own mother howling.

May 30

I had to sit on the steel railroad tracks
to eat my sandwich and you understand I wrapped it
in wax paper since that is as far as I went
in preservation and I remember my serial number
and I was an H in case somebody murdered me
for that was the day we fanned out in all directions
with poppies in one hand and quarters in the other,
the photograph that of a corporal with his balls blown off.

Jack

A suit, a coat, a gabardine,

Bringt arayn dayn Kleinen ziyn

Oswald with his mouth open do you remember that
Ruby Baby one of the wild Jews from East Dallas
a roomful of cops with suits they got from the rack
in Bernie's wholesale house go in the side door
Oswald bent over in pain his mouth open his
gun his gun Ruby Redbreast a 44 long
a sharkskin with a button on the inside pocket
a silk lining a Hart Schaffner & Marx a
rod where a rod should be a mouth as silent as
an ear of corn as a deer with a hole in his heart
now that the Jews were dragged into the assassination.

May Frick Be Damned

In Pittsburgh we used to say, "Tomorrow we strike,
go home, make babies," but always with a Polish
accent and the bars were crowded at ten
in the morning. I for one was stopped once
walking on an empty street downtown
with no reason for being there—I had
three dollars in my pocket so I wasn't
guilty of loitering—may Frick be damned
in Hell forever and ever; may money be stuffed
in all his pockets, may an immigrant
set fire to the money; let Wimpy reign,
"Let's you and him kiss," let love take place
in old cars, let them line up at the curb
in Lover's Lane and let the voyeurs go
from car to car with flashlights, I whisper this.

The Trent Lott,
The MacNamara Blues

I would be happy if one of them would offer his
finger or a piece of his cock and not the usual
sensitive skin by way of remorse and he could
lick the ground while he does it, either one could
go first, it doesn't matter, one could sing his
We Will Overcome, the other could do his
Let's Remember Pearl Harbor but he has to
include the introduction which on hearing
in Woolworth's over and over sitting down
at the Whites Only section in 1941
I memorized but all involuntarily,
or they could lop their arms off as the saints
of Christ did when they lost Jerusalem on
the boats going back to France and tossed them overboard;
and there is a basket just for remorseful limbs
in front of the Library hard by the bored lions
only half a block from W. W. Norton my
publisher I could walk to and sing
for this is what singers are for, little darling.

The Tie

for Mark Hillringhouse

The other time I wore a tie my friend Mark
had called me that Berrigan had died
and there was a funeral at St. Mark's
and Kenneth Koch and John Ashbery were speaking
on his behalf to those who guard the mountain
and though it was a hundred degrees I stopped in
a Goodwill to buy the tie and a jacket as well
which made me look like a priest or a head
waiter at a French restaurant in the upper Fifties,
the tie alone gave such a look of dignity
and even stiffened my neck when it came to lowlife
poets and painters, dozens of whom were there
filling up the pews; and there was a painting by
Alice Neel of Berrigan in an armchair
facing the pews and afterwards we walked, even
sort of marched down Second Avenue to the apartment,
someone in front holding the painting up,
only Berrigan was naked and the fat rolled
over the edge of the armchair and Alice—Alice
Notley—was sitting in the back bedroom
to escape the praises and afterwards Mark and I
walked back to my car and on the way I threw
the tie and jacket into a large wire basket,
my short-sleeved shirt was soaked and we told stories
about his life in the Polish and Ukrainian marshes.

Original Stern Country

Sunday morning I made friends with a king
poodle in a bar on Houston Street,
he was resting on the tiles and panting
so I told *him* my dream, his name was Nero
and he was German to boot, that is, his mistress
was German so I talked to him in *Deutsche*
but after a while I realized I was berating him
because he didn't speak English and my regards
to Hitler, it's not the dog's fault, he's from France
anyhow, though he lives now in Marienbad, I
tell him the movie was horrible, as far as I
remember—I saw it twice—I compared it
to *The Informer,* with Victor McLaughlin which
I saw five times, at least, each time I'm shocked
how short it is, and raw and honest, as if the
actors were being taken hold of by something
huge—and then *à nous la Liberté*—which
predates *Modern Times* as an assault on
the modern worker enslaved even to the point of
identifying sexual love with freedom,
something in the works, a finger, a screwdriver—
the dream was *about* a screwdriver, it took place
in Easton's Center Square since where I live now
it doesn't have a square and anyhow I

only dream about old cities, or maybe it
was a finger. I get lost in my dreams,
dark dirty barren passageways, I say
traum to Nero, I say "trauma," my birthday
is coming up, I'll be travelling in Texas
and sitting down among the uninformed
without a dog, where no one cocks his head
and no black eyes go wild, or I will be toasted
as part of their fund-raising, Nero understands,
his whining is the sound of a violin,
everything is burning, did you notice?

Bolero

So one day when the azalea bush was firing
away and the Japanese maple was roaring I
came into the kitchen full of daylight and
turned on my son's Sony sliding over the
lacquered floor in my stocking feet for it was
time to rattle the cannisters and see what
sugar and barley have come to and how *Bolero*
sounds after all these years and if I'm loyal
still and when did I have a waist that thin?
And if my style was too nostalgic and where
were you when I was burning alive, nightingale?

Dumbbells

I will have dumbbells since the leaf is lean
and I am at the queen's house and I'm sitting
in the sunroom in a wicker chair with
sunshine, so Goddamn your waiting rooms
and travelling centers, Goddamn the train stations,
Goddamn the lines at the market and the scandals,
who did whom, Goddamn the candy, Goddamn
everything. I want dumbbells, watch me go from
twenty-five to forty, I won't raise my shoulders
when I do, Goddamn the governor
Goddamn the president, I will lift fifty pounds, the
bells are round, I hate the discs, I love
the number printed in white, a script, remember
while painting your roof with slime or washing your bricks
or one hand feeding the Chevy and one hand spilling
your pile of precious cards you still have dumbbells.

Stern Country

For sleeplessness, your head face down, your shoulder blades
floating and aspirin as a last resort, when
death is threatening, though lately I have experimented
with numbers and as for dreams I've never been boring
and only once did I bite the arm of a woman
sitting next to me and I should be careful,
she might have a hand-written poem or a memoir
and didn't I bite her arm and aren't we both
poets, though I warn her that I make gurgling
noises and twitch in both legs and make the bed
jump and I am exhausted from looking at poems
and I don't care about her nuts and bolts
and she has to go to the wilderness herself
and fuck the exercises, let her get smashed
by a Mack truck, then she'll be ready to mourn.

Gimbel's

For only three dollars I was able to see
D. H. Lawrence's dirty pictures which
Scotland Yard in its artistic wisdom
let him take to New Mexico provided
he kept them there, something like that, and he was
ordered not to come back to England with a
hard-on or he would face constabulatory wrath
and he was ordered not to piss on concrete
or even the grass that grows between the cracks
but find a splintered telephone pole or a wall
and share his business there with dogs since he
himself was more an animal than a man,
he says so himself, and love belongs in the coal cellar,
I myself have proof of this; I fantasized
when I was thirty or so that the beds at Gimbel's
the rows and rows of them, the tufted, the striped
one morning a week, not to interrupt sales,
not to make anyone nervous, or walk with her head down
or hold her hand on her mouth, would be given over
to public fucking, I would have been so happy.

Worms

Some fisherman, I kept them in a can, only
I was stupido infinito, and they were juicy and
cold moving in segments, I who was one of
them as well as one of him, but I won't
make the same mistake this time, you can bet
your snow drops on that, you can bet your diffodils,
your forsythia weed, your curling hyacinth
holding their stubby fingers up against the freezing
    sun-glare.

Trickle Down

I smelled *my* dead man coming down the hill
on the way to the subway from the Peoples' Convention
though the true stink was in the false promises
and he—or she—was only a memento—
the word my aunt Bess used for metaphor—
and they were made in Spanish and English, the girls
who played with my horror spoke both languages—
if one more person asks me why the police
didn't cart the body away or who was running
in 1980, and what the area is like
today I'll die from boredom as if in America
in the South Bronx what was trickle down
then was different from what is trickle down
now: a mouth is under the faucet, a tongue
is licking a drop of water out of an empty
copper pipe, a dry heart is screaming.

Lilies

Those lilies of the field, one Sunday night
I got caught in Pocono traffic and sat there
for twenty minutes during the which in front
a madman saw me in his mirror and leaped
out of his car and running screamed Dr. Stern
I followed your advice I gave up everything
Thoreau was right simplicity I was your
student the which I stared at him the cars were
starting up again but I no longer
believed and had to leave him stranded, I
love you, I shouted, read something else, I would
have pulled off the side of the road but there was no
shoulder there and so I lost him, whatever his
name was. I made a sharp left turn and that was
that, but what I owe him in his under
shirt, how long his beard was then, his eyes
were blue, his tires were bald, what Christ owes me!

Loyal Carp

I myself a bottom feeder I knew what
a chanson à la carp was I a lover
of carp music for I heard carp singing
behind the glass on the Delaware River,
keeping the shad themselves company
and always it was a basso, in that range there
was space for a song compleat, it was profundo
enough and just to stop and drink in that
melody and just to hum behind those
whiskers, that was muck enough for my life.

Golden Rule

My Blue Jay

All she wants is for you to stay away from her egg
and all she wants is for you to shut up when it comes
to the three things she hates the most: justice,
mercy, humility. She detests Jesus and she can define
what he is, and was, and wants to be while flying
unbearably low by the one word, "squawk"; and
that is why I pulled my straw hat down over
my bald head and that is why my orange cat
almost died with fear and why she won
the argument with her big black shadow while resting only
    on one leg.

City of God

It takes longer now than it used to take
and I am tempted to climb the back stairs
which have two risers less than the front ones and
it comes to thirteen rather than coming to fifteen
though they are curved, which adds a lateral motion
to the blood-starved thigh, making up in cunning
what it lacks in slope and there at the top
instead of a bald and flaking mirror you almost
walk inside of, a book that you trip over,
The City of God, him and a snake on the cover
starring at each other, the snake with an eye
that's mostly film, the saint's half-crossed, the two
are so close together, and they are arguing
about my future, and one of them argues in Greek
outside my bedroom, down the sloping hallway.

The Taste of Ducklings

That's the stick I made a marsh for and leaned
two rocks against, the one that lived through snow
and cat piss and dish towels, and those are the neighbors I
    hate
though I love their dog and that is the sky I brought into
my kitchen, including the clouds, and the turtle that loves
the taste of ducklings, he swims under water, and that is
the bush that hides everything there against the
chain-link fence, the thing I loved dragged through
the mud, though mud is just dirt and water
and nothing more—just try ascribing a soul
to water and dirt, just try blowing your meat-filled
breath on what your hands made, bomb-crazed lunatic.

L'Chaim

There goes that toast again, four chipped
glasses full of some kind of ruby held up
to the sun this time, death crumbs falling and rising
like dust-motes, fish eggs, bubbles, here's to you, bubbles,
here's to Mardi Gras, here's to the apple tree
pinned against my fence, here's to reproach,
here's to doing it to music, here's to fog,
and here's to fog again, and life dividing
inside the fog; oh when it dissipates
let's make a circle; here's to the baby hiding
inside his clothes, here's to his being
alive without me, here's to the mountain again,
for what the hell, I might as well be on the mountain,
here's to delectables, free health care, love, popcorn.

Cigars

The same cracked hoarse nasal sexy laugh—
I almost lifted my face out of the newspaper
to remind her of the drowned bee and the shaky
pedestrian bridge, I almost told her her
favorite passage of Mahler, we were that close
going up and down the ladders and interchanging
souls with each other, we were that overlapping,
appearing and disappearing, that prayerful,
lighting each other's cigars inside the room of laurel-green
    horse laughter.

Good Boy

An awful thing to do to a dog, tie a
blue lead around his face, say sit,
click your cricket, say good boy and give
him a treat; an awful thing to do to a man,
close the factory when he turns sixty-five
and let him row across the river on Social
Security alone; I sat on the porch
moaning for nothing or walked down my mud path
through the hordes of geese, their crap *partout*
and no one with a small white plastic baggie
to save the day, and I was followed and hissed at
since geese know and are aggressive sometimes
beyond the issue of bread. You know the guard,
he who lowered his head and opened his mouth
to show his red throat? He saved my life.

111

Harold and 1

For the record there are two trees that followed
me most of my life and they are now in the dirt
left of the cedar fence when I stare out
from the east, the bedroom window with the red
and white quilt on the long wall and I won't
shame them by telling how or where I retrieved them
and what the bucket was I carried them in
or how I watered them three whole days not counting
the rain or how I mollycoddled them
several new ways, though when I left it grew
windy after the boy William quit on me
when he got a job, he says, changing tires,
one of the more disgraceful and filthy jobs,
so I had to tie a string between three sticks
so the new cutter would see how they grew there
and not commit murder as he walked back and forth
doing his rows and knowing I made a choice—
the strings would tell him that—between the weeds
and the thorny trees, though the weeds were beautiful—
but anyhow the whacker jumped and I was
relieved of half my culture nor could I berate
the new cutter, it was so hot, his name
was Harold and we were two misty figures
living in water, and struggling inside three pieces

of string, though one was cut, we stood *between*
the two, Harold and I, and we were stumped
for a minute, our theories almost bogged down, the
    whacker
was leaping in his hands, on his black face
on my Jewish, the goodness and mercy depended.

Shouldering

We were surrounded by buttercup and phlox
so you know what the month was, one of us had
Sarah Vaughn in her inner ear, one of us
Monk, who put a table there we didn't
know but we were more or less grateful nor was it
even chained to anything and the eggs we
ate were perfect, I cracked them on my head
as I always do and shattered them with my fist,
the grape tomatoes which only cost a dollar
a pint were almost acid-free, the tire
was growing softer but I was a veteran
of *real* tires, and bumper jacks, I even go
back to steaming radiators, I could
tell you things, I said to Monk, I walked
two miles once with a half-gallon of gas
leaking out of an orange juice carton, "In My
Solitude" he said, "September Song," said she.

Bejewels

It were the ink splats from a writing machine
I bought so many centuries ago I
hardly could lift it down from the luggage rack
along with my socks and such, for while the others
converted to braille I stuck with the splats, I didn't
even do *la touche,* the period in between that
lasted thirty years, I stuck with splats
although I were growing old by then and I said
"what" too many times but you should see me
floating on the horse turds first, then walking
deep in the thorns, then balancing on top
of the barbed wire for just to say I love you,
not to mention the heather there on the rocks
an hour north of Galway, and putting it down
on the coffee table with my other bejewels there.

My Sister's Funeral

Since there was no mother for the peach tree we did it
all alone, which made the two of us closer
though closeness brought its loneliness, and it would
have been better I think sometimes to be sterile
from the start just to avoid the pain
which in my life this far has lasted seventy
years for I am in love with a skeleton
on whose small bones a dress hung for a while,
on whose small skull a bit of curly hair
was strung, and what is dust I still don't know
since there was no mother to turn to then and ask
what else was she wearing, did she have on shoes,
and were the two trees from Georgia, and was it
true somebody said the other peach
should have died instead of her; and I could
imagine the nose going first though forty years later
the trees were still there and not as big as you'd think;
and it was my cousin Red with the flabby lips
who said it, he had red eyes, a red monstrosity,
a flabby body, half the house was filled with
male cousins, they were born in rooms a
short distance from the rats, I can't remember
which ones had the accents nor what his
Hebrew name was, nor his English.

The Red Is Fuschia

The red is fuschia growing on the rock
behind the grasses I call toothpicks, the other
is fuschia too though it is orange, just another
wave of the sun, I find a seat after moving
two or three times, the bay on one side, the cleft
tree on the other, all this to keep from dying,
but my main job is keeping the sun out of
my eyes, for this I lower my lids and hold
my hand up to my forehead, it is hard
being this close to a star, for which I wear
a thick black shirt—a theory I have—carved
lines in my forehead, waves sort of, a curved
shadow across my head, a kind of brush stroke,
fat at the neck just gone forever, the wind
in the hair like lines of nobility, the lower lip
about to speak; I have the proof in my hands.

Bio

What it was like to sit with Mr. Fox
on the Blvd. Raspail and negotiate
my post at Morlais, then Toulouse, then come back
in a riveted trunk with Henry Millers sewn
into my lining, Frank Sinatra to greet me
in the mile square city, Dutch ships everywhere,
my father and mother in from Pittsburgh to give me
my French lesson, my fiancée pulling me down,
the mayor of New York god knows who, the president
asinine again, the dove I loved
in an army boot size eleven and a half and
dove or not, dove feathers or not, blood staining
the white chest, a cascade of snow come pouring
from the spruce's upper limbs, cascade, waterfall,
sheet, blanket, my mountain, your roof, your dovecote,
eating fish on the *Times,* 103rd Street,
Zoey in a corset, even then she
was a throwback—I have unlaced a corset,
and at a vanity I have sat on a stained
bench and broken my knees against art dreco
peeling wood, and there among the powders
and creams and rouges I have read Montaigne,
Locke and Hobbes, and since it was there, I read
the rituals of the Eastern Star and studied
my face in the unsilvered mirror, what about you?

Moon

This is what happened on the dark side of the moon
he thought was Roquefort and lollygagging eternal
for he didn't have a chance, nor did his sister
win the lawsuit with Squibb, thus giving them
a farm for their old age in upstate New York
where he could read the *Times* in the county library
and stand in line for cheese and once a week
have an early-bird special at Bickford's
and spend mornings studying the bald leghorns
in their front yard; and it was a far cry from
Oklahoma as it was a cry monstrous
from the valley of Mott Street where he drank his coffee
with a tablespoon poking his eye out
and walked across town to a desk he rented to write
his poems, for such was New York, and he was delivered
by radiation and injected with Lupton
and barely could walk, and for his lunch at Tony's
he only had a five dollar bill for his check was
coming Tuesday, though he was telling the truth and
once you reach a certain age the food could
be anything for the talk comes first and days like
that the moon is out in the afternoon
and Saturn or Neptune, I forget which, has not yet
appeared in just propinquity for it's not

dark but only the darkest of dark blue
even on Mott Street, even on Houston, across
from the flea and the parking lot, my own monstrous.

Battle of the Bulge

The way a fly who dies in sugar water,
he couldn't find a way to lift his wings
out of there, they were so heavy, the way
a plant doesn't need that rich a dirt, the way
it chokes from too much love, the way
I lay on the ground, I dug a hip hole, I slept
with grass, and dirt, the way Ammon Hennacy
wore a red flannel shirt, and a tie, he was
Dorothy Day's friend—you knew the saint?—it was
my own costume for years, he was in prison
with Berkman—in Atlanta—Berkman was there
for shooting and stabbing Frick, Hennacy for
conscience; I met Hennacy on Spruce Street
in 1958, the same year I met
Jack Lindeman who lost his hearing in Belgium,
the winter of 1944, he lives in
Fleetwood, P.A. and we communicate by
fax—I never heard him ask for pity
nor did we ever talk about that winter, he
introduced me to Dorothy Day and published
his poems in the *Catholic Worker*—and Marvin Hadburg,
he whom *I* pity, he was drafted when the
government was desperate and sent to
southern Georgia for four weeks training

and then to Bastogne three days before Christmas
where he spent a week in a barn and came home
with both feet frozen a day or two short of two months
some of the flesh cut off, as I remember,
a gold discharge button in his lapel,
selling underwear again in his father's store,
his head very small, his shoulders hunched, his mouth
always open—I would say he was a
collector of feathers for the Achaean archer
Teucer of the incurved bow, whose shoulder
Hector smashed with a rock, just where the clavicle
leads over to the neck and breast, thus deadening
his wrist and fingers, I would say that Ajax
knocked him down when passing by and Zeus,
deflector of arrows and breaker of spears, the father
of slaughter without end, he pissed on him.

Mars

What you say bout Orson Welles his folly, his
belly full of sheepskin, liquid of ale?
What you say bout the cave on the bluff my father oh
were packing us up one night at the end of the thirties
he knew as a child-child dark-skinned Jewish bastard
he had *smoked* there tobeys you know and lukewarm
RC Cola, child-child roasted potato,
and I came home from the movie at 10 o'clock
and he was packing and she for they was crazy
for caves and oh them Martians and ah them Martians,
and I saw Orson in 1950 in Paris oh,
he was directing a play and he was fat-fat
and ah he bade us welcome and how did we know?
and was it Macbeth? Child-child in 1950
for I love *Touch of Evil* best and worst-worst
Citizen Kane of California, Hearst-Hearst.

Thought

After he left I turned to my cold soup
for I was starving after so much talk,
and as a precaution I pulled the blind down and took
the phone off the hook, and I was using a spoon
that had to belong to an earl once, a pink
pig he had to be, for there was a spot of
pink in the heraldry, and it was three days
old and the meat was too fat but I can't start
doing that now; and as for music I turned
to one of the B's, and as for Thought—and you know
what I mean by Thought—oh prune, oh apple
with the flesh exposed too long, I turned to the beaver
who, by his chewing, given the way he chews,
and by the sapling he abandoned there in
the low-lying bush above my water I knew
he had to leave and his thinking was interrupted,
although he changed my river and brought the birds
out in his wake, and with his wooden chips,
one of which I carry to prophesize,
he made a dry path for his murderers.

Desnos

regards to Bill Kulik

I considered the bourgeois virtues for one day
and it was my birthday when on a Wednesday morning
the palmist who walked among the corpses in Buchenwald
was sent on his journey by the Gestapo in Paris,
he, the dreamer of WXYZ,
he, the friend of Chico Marx and Bert Williams;
so much for thrift, hard work, piety and patriotism,
so much for not spending the principal and for the
      argument
against gratification and the argument for, and guess
how the light shone on my grandfather's stick and guess
what it was he carried in his dry mouth.

Plank Road

You don't know what a plank road is, you macadam
person you—you think they couldn't lay wood for
thirty miles, and how would it be when the carriages
ran over it, and wouldn't there be grooves, and what about
the early automobiles and when those nails ah loosened
then oh the rattle and oh the bump and the echoes, but
me I have been disengaged and February being
what it is I have divided my century
into four parts and I have talked to my shadow,
it being the day, it being the night, and there was
snow up to the armpits and touching your tongue
to a metal Pontiac you froze there, for starters.

Driven

The only star last night was cloud-riven,
a frog said that to me, but aside from the word
"riven," which could have been "rivet" or "privet,"
for sometimes he disguises his voice, that puffed-up
goggle-eyed bug-eating monster, a machine of
sorts sitting on a pod and floating south the
way a frog floats south and he half looks
himself, and if you ask him he goes on, for
he is *driven,* I prefer it, that *driven,*
try that under your cloud, or in your big mouth,
along with steak and eggs; he says driven,
and stars are driven too, some are cloud-driven,
and some are clear and one is blue and under that
blue star I slept then I woke up
driven—I was a little dizzy, and staggered
here and there but I was driven—ah
cut his legs off and grill them, eat in the weeds
and grow two hearts, two lungs, another eye,
give yourself up for dissection, call it hiven,
better than heaven, spiders, moths, flies, frog-hiven.

Twenty-Five Cents

How did he know it was me and I would deal
with him on the metal bridge all new going over
and back and I understood of all those tourists just
where he stood and we both had pockets, that was for
sure, and I couldn't tell if he was the father or
grandfather for his skin was ruined and his head
was shaved and his English was so original we both
turned to Spanish and the little girl had to be
eleven maybe or she could be eight and just
tall, and bright, and she was his equal and spoke
both languages perfectly thus making me feel
like a kind of ape who never would learn the verbs and
genders, how did it start, but I wouldn't budge
and he almost wept as if I had lost a house I
could have had for the asking or I could have had
a rare car, a Bugatti, a Duesenberg,
and I was fighting for pennies, pennies, shame on the
Spanish, shame on the Jews, we could have been
in-laws too, and think of the food I'd miss,
and hunting the calf's ear, where he came from the game
of choice, come his *Novembre*; remember me,
it's been my bridge for over six years, I lost
my head here once but I lost more, oh scarred
and ravished father, oh sacrificed daughter.

Brain of Magellan

She would be in her forties now and her mother
I know is dead and her mother's lover, the wife
of my closest friend is dead, and he is dead
too, oh all of them, from butter
or cigarettes or elevators or just shit
in the New York sky, 125th and
Riverside Drive, it was the first time
for the girl and both her mothers, and we were living
along the river just far enough from the nearest
city to see the sky as a sheet of stars
alive and pulsing the way it gets and after
supper we all went out on the porch and the girl
began to scream for she had never seen the
stars like that, given the haze or just given
the lights of the city, it was a sky abounding
in information, and the brain of Magellan
practically everywhere, my screaming astronomer
caught in the burning sky underneath *his* burning.

Shepherd

Greece, the light of my life, but there was a man who
taught Business and one day an ex-student
from another college came to see him and she was
gorgeous enough you wanted to die, and after
thirty minutes alone they both came out
and how he sucked his pipe I could have murdered him;
but he was critical for she lay on a hillside
above new Samos and woke up to a bell for
there was a shepherd and there was a dog and after
how many minutes he fucked her with the dog
barking, and *how disgusting* my colleague said,
imagine, a filthy shepherd, and I was stunned
by the word "shepherd," it meant nothing to him;
and what the sun was like that morning, the marble
she fingered the while oh two or three thousand years
there baking and freezing, but most of all I hated
how I had to accept his version of a formal
rift in order to fight him, how I retreated
behind some broken stones, a fireplace, say,
four hundred years old, and we would have to argue
about sulfa and penicillin, I wanted to
pull the pipe out of his mouth, I wanted to
have a dog like that, a bell either tied
to his white throat or at my own neck playing
Schubert or Mahler, down on my worn out knees.

Corsets

I was caught in a time warp there in my landlady's
basement apartment struggling with her niece's corset
the which at a dinner party I was instructed by
the woman sitting next to me that *girdles* were the style
in the early fifties, not corsets, but it was a time warp
and even though she was young she came from Corfu
and even though it was 1950 they still wore
corsets there as they did in America in
1930 or even in 1920
among the healthy and flapperless, and I
unhooked her since there were more ways of surrendering
then for she was studying Greek at Hunter College
and I was writing poems of pure endearment
tinged with touches of Utopia that came
from all the places you'd expect, and since I
associated Utopias already with corsets,
having written perfectly at my mother's vanity
amid the perfumes and powders, half sitting on a
wobbly bench on top of *her* corset I confounded
one kind of love with another the way you always
did—and do—land of milk, land of honey.

Sacco, Vanzetti

I have asked ten Italians at my beloved's
father's and mother's fiftieth wedding anniversary
at the Rainbow Room and not one of the ten
knew though it was the moment of Italian triumph
greater than Toscanini, greater than La Guardia;
and I have a personal hero, Judge Musmanno,
who spent twenty years proving their innocence,
a good shoe maker and a poor fish peddler,
never dreaming to steal, never to assassinate,
for whom I fight back tears and quanch my heart,
trobling to my throat to not weep before them,
whom I do love and who I would have marched for,
who taught me for to talk to scorning men
in rooms the size of bathrooms or small stadiums,
trobling to my own bosses and even friends,
since spit came first and drops of learning too
like slow-falling snow the day before spring
seventy-seven years later for whom not a stamp,
not a square, not a statue, anywhere to behold,
nor a text, nor a wall of labored steel for to remember
our helpless shame, their murder, tenors, sopranos.

Whoso

Whoso lives in a town that had a stone jail
and went there because of a fishbone in his throat
although the jail was small and had two stories
only and a fire escape for kindness, he
argued with the mayor for he didn't have anyone
to plead for him; and since he had Tourette's he
shouted *fuck you* to justice and explained it was
a salmon and how its bones were spread and where he
started chewing once it was cooked and the red had
flaked; and he still haunted the jail forty years
after it closed and loved its stones and even
got permission to go inside though there was
nothing anymore, only a storeroom
for old ledgers and voting boxes the fingers
had smoothed as they caressed the two parties,
brave and stupid from the start, nor were there
any bars left nor were there shackles and he could
have taken a streetcar anywhere
once he walked through the door, for though it was only
four decades ago it was more like the
nineteenth century, there was more air then, and there was
space to lie against the wicker seats and
just think, or he could walk up his favorite alley
and stop to lean against a tree and whistle

a third higher than two of the three birds there,
a fugue of sorts, the fishbone in his throat
suddenly gone, the dogs liberated.

Homesick

I was reading again and French apples
were on my mind and oranges the way they sold them
in giant carts and how the skin was thick and
loosened from the flesh and how it made an
orange saucer where you placed the sections
after you pulled the threads away, the ugly word
"pith," it's called, and raspberries with cream—
and how it would have been if I had stayed
in the same hotel another eight or ten years and
married someone else—it always comes to
that—and taken up another trade,
for as you know what we call nostalgia
is for the life we *didn't* live, so much for
homesickness, and I am homesick too for
southern Spain, where I didn't live, but mostly for
Mogador (where I didn't live) with the tiny
white streets and blue shutters, one store the
flutes on one side, the drums on the other, the synagogue
smaller than the African Methodist church
on North Governor Street in Iowa City
before they rounded us up, though we had two days,
for we had spies, to tear the linings open
and sew our jewels in and our thousand franc notes,
although we had to leave our heavy furniture

behind, and Libby's picture, when we boarded
the plane for Paris, more like the camel that took us
to live with the Berbers in the Atlas mountains
twenty-five hundred years ago than not like,
all of whose fault it was that Ezra who preached
the ups and downs; and how the Berbers welcomed us,
and how the French put us in crowded rooms
and made us sit for hours, for they believed in
égalité, so everyone should die of
boredom equally and *Vive La France* and
Hail to the Eagle and Rah, Miss Liberty,
one of her breasts exposed—I have nostalgia
for your life too, what are you, Mongolian?
Don't leave the rugs behind, milk the horses!
Are you a Russian? You are great at this.
Light the samovar! I give you my past for
nothing. Here is your number. Line up, my lovers!

The Law

The world is always burning, you should fly
from the burning if you can, and you should hold
your head oh either above or below the dust
and you should be careful in the blocks of Bowery
below or above the Broome that always is changing
from one kind of drunkenness to another
for that is the law of suffering, and you know it.

She Was a Dove

For Anne Marie

Red are her eyes, for she was a dove once,
and green was her neck and blue and gray her throat,
croon was her cry and noisy flutter her wing once
going for water, or reaching up for another note.

And yellow her bill, though white some, and red her feet
though not to match her eyes for they were more suave,
those feet, and he who bore down above her
his feathers dropped around her like chaff from wheat.

And black was her mood, consider a dove that black,
as if some avian fury had overcome her
and overtaken my own oh lackadaisical state
for she was the one I loved and I abused her.

Blue we lived in, blue was our country seat,
and wrote our letters out on battered plates
and fought injustice and once or twice French-kissed there
and took each other out on desperate dates.

And it was a question always should we soar—
like eagles you know—or should we land and stay,
the battle I fought for sixty years or more
and still go over every day.

And there was a spot of orange above the bone
that bore a wing, though I could never explain
how that was what I lived and died for
or that it blossomed in the brain.

Notes

"E.P. I"

Ferdie and Fordie: reference to the novelist Ford Maddox Ford, important to Ezra Pound during the English Years.

Dancing Nancy: several times in the Cantos, Pound—out of nowhere—asks the question, "Where art thou now, Nancy?"

"E.P. II"

Tom Valasek was a fellow teacher of mine at the time of Pound's death.

"Those Are Saucers That Were His Eyes"

The title refers to *Little Orphan Annie*, weird old comic strip. Sandy was Annie's dog.

"Dog That I Am"

Skinker is a street in St. Louis.

"Sylvia"

Sylvia refers to Sylvia Stern, my older sister, dead in 1933, at age nine.

"Just Say Goodbye to Mother"

The title is the name of a sentimental American song from the Spanish-American War of 1898.

"May 30"

May 30th is Memorial Day, in memory of American soldiers killed in various wars.

H was the symbol on dog tags worn by American Jewish soldiers during WWII.

"Jack"

Jack refers to Jack Ruby, killer of Lee Harvey Oswald. The italicized lines are in Yiddish, from a racy, comic song of the thirties and forties, "A suit, a coat, a gabardine, / Bring in your small son."

"May Frick Be Damned"

In the comic strip *Popeye*, Wimpy used to say, "Let's you and him fight."

"The Tie"

Alice Notley, the poet, was Ted Berrigan's wife.

"Trickle Down"

The Peoples' Convention, a radical leftist gathering, was held in the South Bronx in 1980. Both Reagan and Carter made their false promises there.

"Loyal Carp"

The poem refers to a glass enclosure at the forks of the Delaware and Lehigh Rivers in Easton, PA where the shad can be closely observed fighting their way upstream to mate.

"Bio"

Mr. Renaud (Fox) was the French minister of education in 1950.

"Battle of the Bulge"

Alexander Berkman was a famous anarchist at the beginning of the twentieth century and Emma Goldman's lover.

"Mars"

The poem refers to the "War of the Worlds," Orson Welles's famous radio show, airing in 1938. Huge numbers of people believed we were being attacked by Martians.

"Sacco, Vanzetti"

The italicized lines—somewhat re-composed, are from Bartolomeo Vanzetti's last letter, quoted in John Dos Passos, Dorothy Day and elsewhere. I am inspired in some of my own lines by Vanzetti's language and his spirit. He learned to read and write English while waiting to be executed by the state of Massachusetts, in August, 1927.

Credits

Poems in this volume have appeared or will appear in the following journals: *American Poetry Review*: "La Pergola," "E.P. I," "E.P. III," "The 18th Book Fair," "Albatross I," "Those Are Saucers That Were His Eyes," "The Gulls," "The Tie," "Lilies"; *Atlantic Monthly*: "Loyal Carp"; *Blackbird*: "Just Say Goodbye to Mother," "May 30"; *Boulevard*: "Jack," "May Frick Be Damned," "Harold and I"; *Courtland Review*: "Twenty-Five Cents," "Plank Road"; *Ecotone*: "Gimbel's," "Desnos," "Homesick"; *5AM*: "The Trent Lott, The MacNamara Blues"; *Georgia Review*: "Tenderness," "My Sister's Funeral," "L'Chaim"; *Iowa Review*: "The Red Is Fuschia," "Thought," "Sacco, Vanzetti"; *Lyric*: "A Google of Geese," "The Cup"; *Maggid*: "L'Chaim," "Desnos," "City of God," "Golden Rule," "Taste of Ducklings," "Soup," "Battle of the Bulge"; *Margie*: "Good Boy" (previously titled "The Guard"); *The New Yorker*: "Sylvia," "Stern Country," "Never Went to Birdland," "She Was a Dove," "Cigars"; *Nightsun*: "Whoso"; *One Trick Pony*: "Trickle Down"; *Ploughshares:* "Bio," "The Law"; *Poetry*: "Bolero"; *Poetry International*: "Original Stern Country"; *Provincetown Arts*: "Shepherd."

"Dog That I Am" appeared in *The Best American Poetry 2004*, edited by David Lehman and Lyn Hejinian, published by Scribner.

"Suzanne" appeared in *Never Before: Poems About First Experiences*, edited by Laure-Anne Bosselaar and published by Four Way Books (2004).